EXTREME MACHINES

by Ian Stevens

Consultant: Alison Howard

BEARPORT
PUBLISHING COMPANY, INC.
New York, New York

Picture credits (t=top; b=bottom; c=center; l=left; r=right): Alvey and Towers: 8-9 all, 10-11 all, 12-13 all, 14-15 all, 18-19 all. Aviation Picture Library: 26b. Corbis: 22-23 all, 24-25 all. Fast Car Photo Library: 27 all. JAMSTEC: 6-7 all. NASA: 16-17 all, 20-21 all. Water Sports Photo Library: 26t.

Every effort has been made to trace the copyright holders, and we apologize in advance for any unintentional omissions. We would be pleased to insert the appropriate acknowledgments in any subsequent edition of this publication.

Library of Congress Cataloging-in-Publication Data
Stevens, Ian, 1958-
  Extreme machines / by Ian Stevens.
    p. cm.—(Top 10s)
  Includes index.
  ISBN 1-59716-065-2 (library binding)—ISBN 1-59716-102-0 (pbk.)
  1. Machinery—Juvenile literature. I. Title. II. Series.

TJ147.S745 2006
629.04—dc22

2005012759

For more information, write to Bearport Publishing Company, Inc., 101 Fifth Avenue, Suite 6R, New York, New York 10003. Printed in the United States of America.

2 3 4 5 6 7 8 9 10

CONTENTS

Introduction.. 4

Shinkai 6500 (No.10) 6

V-22 Osprey Tiltrotor (No. 9) 8

LCAC Hovercraft (No. 8) 10

Thrust SSC (No. 7)................................12

USS *Louisiana* (No. 6) 14

SpaceShipOne (No. 5) 16

TGV Duplex (No. 4) 18

Lockheed SR-71 (No. 3)......................... 20

Antonov An-225 Mriya (No. 2) 22

USS *Ronald Reagan* (No. 1)................... 24

Close But Not Close Enough 26

Stats.. 28

Glossary 30

Index... 32

INTRODUCTION

Machines make our lives easier. We can travel quickly in cars and trains. We can fly on planes to countries that are thousands of miles away. We can sail across oceans on ships. Some machines, however, are like no others. They are bigger, faster, or more powerful than all the rest. This book presents the Top 10 most extreme machines ever built. Each machine was rated on a scale of one to ten in the following categories:

FEATURES We included the most interesting details we could find out about each machine. Which extreme machine is as powerful as 1,000 Ford Escorts? Which machine was made using more than a billion parts? The answers are in this book.

NO. 5 — SPACESHIP-ONE

SpaceShipOne is the world's first privately owned and operated spacecraft. This record-breaking rocket is carried to the edge of space by a jet called White Knight. SpaceShipOne then separates from this jet. The pilot starts the rocket's engine to continue the craft's flight into space.

SPEED
SpaceShipOne can reach a top speed of 2,500 miles per hour (4,023 kph).

FEATURES
The fuel of SpaceShipOne is a mix of laughing gas and rubber. The rocket's wings can fold up to help it glide safely back to Earth.

SpaceShipOne is the first non-government spacecraft to fly at a height of over 60 miles (97 km).

16

SPEED

This category looks at the top speed of each machine. Some machines do not need to go fast to do their work. Other machines were built to break world records.

SIZE

Many of the machines we chose are huge. Other machines are not so large. The more extreme the size, the more points the machine was given.

SIZE

When compared to a rocket, this little craft is tiny. SpaceShipOne weighs just 1.2 tons (1 metric ton).

POWER

SpaceShipOne's single rocket engine produces 96,973 horsepower.

EXTREME SCORES

This extreme machine is a step ahead in the race to conquer space.

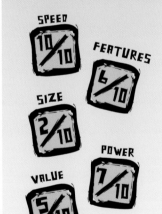

POWER

This section looks at how the machine works, and its power. This measurement is often given in **horsepower**. We also included details about the machine's engine and fuel.

VALUE

SpaceShipOne rocketed into history at a cost of $20 million.

SpaceShipOne was released by White Knight 9 miles (14 km) above Earth's surface.

VALUE

This category covers how much it cost to develop the machine, and whether it was worth the money.

Built in Japan, the Shinkai 6500 is a **submersible** used for deep-sea research around the world. On August 11, 1989, it dove to a record-breaking depth of 4 miles (6 km). This dive was the deepest ever achieved by a **manned** submersible.

SPEED

The **maximum** speed of the Shinkai 6500 is 2.5 **knots**. The machine's deep-sea research does not require it to travel at high speeds.

FEATURES

The Shinkai 6500 can take a crew of three to the bottom of the ocean. It has a very strong shell to withstand the pressure at these great depths.

SIZE

The Shinkai 6500 is 31 feet (9 m) long and 9 feet (3 m) wide. It weighs a massive 25.8 tons (23.4 metric tons).

Shinkai 6500 is used to research the ocean floors of the world.

POWER

This submersible is brought to its dive site and lowered into the sea. It then runs on batteries that last for about 12 hours.

VALUE

The Shinkai 6500 cost $100 million. Each dive costs a further $30,000. The research it does, including earthquake prediction, could be priceless.

This submersible's shell is made from strong titanium.

The Shinkai 6500 is costly and heavy. However, it can go where no other submersible can go.

SPEED 2/10

FEATURES 3/10

SIZE 4/10

POWER 3/10

VALUE 7/10

= TOTAL SCORE 19/50

V-22 OSPREY TILTROTOR

The **V-22** is a dream come true. It takes off and lands like a helicopter. However, it flies like a plane. The **V-22** was developed for the **U.S. Marine Corps.** It was built to bring troops and equipment from ships to land bases.

SPEED

The V-22 has a top speed of 316 miles per hour (509 kph). This is twice as fast as a helicopter.

FEATURES

When the V-22 lands on a ship's deck, its wings and blades can fold up. The V-22 can take off in smaller spaces than a plane. It can fly farther and faster than a helicopter.

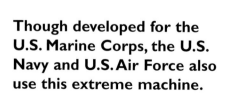

Though developed for the U.S. Marine Corps, the U.S. Navy and U.S. Air Force also use this extreme machine.

The V-22 can take off without a runway, just like a helicopter.

SIZE

This unique **aircraft** weighs around 15 tons (14 metric tons). It can carry a total load of 15,000 pounds (6,804 kg), including 24 Marines.

POWER

Each **propeller** on the V-22 is driven by an engine that can produce 6,150 horsepower.

VALUE

This amazing aircraft comes with the sky-high price tag of $80 million.

The V-22 flies twice as far and twice as fast as a helicopter.

SPEED
6/10

FEATURES
4/10

SIZE
3/10

POWER
5/10

VALUE
7/10

= TOTAL SCORE
25/50

The **LCAC (Landing Craft Air Cushion) Hovercraft** is the only **amphibious** machine on our list. It was developed for the U.S. Navy. It is used to carry troops and equipment at high speeds from ship to shore. This amazing hovercraft can reach more than **70 percent of the world's coastlines.**

SPEED

The LCAC has a top speed of more than 46 miles per hour (74 kph).

FEATURES

This mighty hovercraft has a flat bottom and is made from aluminium. It has four engines. Two of the engines force air under the LCAC to lift it off land or water.

SIZE

This giant land-and-water machine can carry up to 68 tons (62 metric tons). It weighs more than 120 tons (109 metric tons) when fully loaded.

The LCAC can land in difficult conditions.

POWER

Four gas engines provide 16,000 horsepower.

VALUE

The LCAC carries a price tag of $25 million. It was used to carry **critical** aid to victims of the Asian tsunami in 2004.

LCAC can carry huge loads at high speeds.

The LCAC can go places that other vehicles just can't reach.

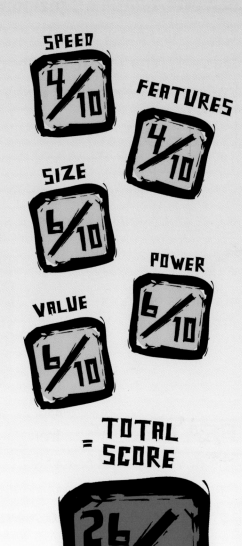

SPEED
4/10

FEATURES
4/10

SIZE
6/10

POWER
6/10

VALUE
6/10

= TOTAL SCORE
26/50

Thrust **SSC** (**Supersonic** Car) is the fastest and most powerful car ever built. This jet-powered machine was designed to go faster than the speed of sound. On October 15, 1997, at Black Rock Desert, Nevada, it reached the record-breaking speed of 766 miles per hour (1,233 kph).

SPEED

Thrust's top speed is 850 miles per hour (1,368 kph). It can go from 0–100 miles per hour (0–161 kph) in 4 seconds. It reached 600 miles per hour (966 kph) in just 16 seconds.

FEATURES

The driver enters Thrust SSC through the roof. The vehicle is as powerful as 145 Formula One racing cars, or 1,000 Ford Escorts.

Thrust SSC is the first car to break the sound barrier.

POWER

The Thrust SSC has two jet engines. They produce a combined force totaling 110,000 horsepower.

Thrust SSC uses a parachute braking system to slow down. Here are the parachute launchers viewed head on.

Supersonic speed and incredible power make Thrust SSC a really extreme machine.

SPEED
8/10

FEATURES
6/10

SIZE
2/10

POWER
8/10

VALUE
3/10

= TOTAL SCORE
27/50

SIZE

Thrust SSC weighs 10 tons (9 metric tons). It is 54 feet (16 m) long.

VALUE

The car took about 100,000 hours to build. Today, it would cost about $10 million to make this supersonic machine.

The **USS** *Louisiana* is the largest **ballistic submarine** ever built for the **U.S. Navy.** It carries 24 Trident **nuclear missiles** that can be fired very quickly. The submarine was named after the eighteenth state of the **United States.**

SPEED

This massive submarine patrols the sea at a speed of about 20 knots. It is fast enough to outrun most enemy craft.

FEATURES

The USS *Louisiana* has one propeller. The submarine is powered by a **nuclear reactor**. It can run for more than 15 years before it needs more fuel.

SIZE

The USS *Louisiana* is 561 feet (171 m) long. It weighs about 18,750 tons (17,010 metric tons).

The USS *Louisiana* **was the last Trident submarine built.**

The USS *Louisiana* remains active today.

POWER

The submarine's nuclear reactor is capable of producing a massive 60,000 horsepower.

VALUE

The USS *Louisiana* cost $12 million to develop. Its main purpose is to defend.

This nuclear-powered machine is the most expensive submarine ever built.

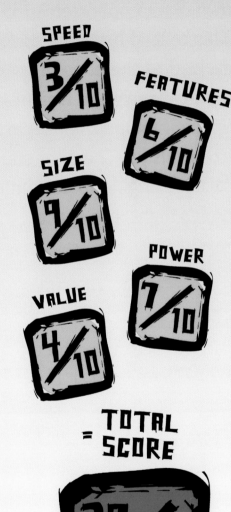

SPEED
3/10

FEATURES
6/10

SIZE
9/10

POWER
7/10

VALUE
4/10

= TOTAL SCORE
29/50

SpaceShipOne is the world's first privately owned and operated spacecraft. This record-breaking rocket is carried to the edge of space by a jet called White Knight. SpaceShipOne then separates from this jet. The pilot starts the rocket's engine to continue the craft's flight into space.

SPEED

SpaceShipOne can reach a top speed of 2,500 miles per hour (4,023 kph).

FEATURES

The fuel of SpaceShipOne is a mix of laughing gas and rubber. The rocket's wings can fold up to help it glide safely back to Earth.

SpaceShipOne is the first non-government spacecraft to fly at a height of over 60 miles (97 km).

SIZE

When compared to a rocket, this little craft is tiny. SpaceShipOne weighs just 1.2 tons (1 metric ton).

POWER

SpaceShipOne's single rocket engine produces 96,973 horsepower.

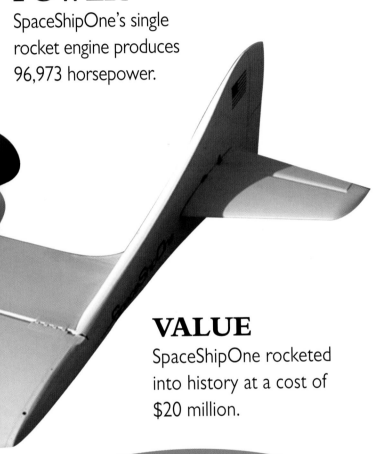

VALUE

SpaceShipOne rocketed into history at a cost of $20 million.

SpaceShipOne was released by White Knight 9 miles (14 km) above Earth's surface.

This extreme machine is a step ahead in the race to conquer space.

SPEED 10/10

FEATURES 6/10

SIZE 2/10

POWER 7/10

VALUE 5/10

= TOTAL SCORE

30/50

The **TGV Duplex** is one of the world's fastest trains. It is run by **TGV**, the French railway company. Nicknamed the "workhorse," this high-speed train travels mainly between **Paris** and **Lyon**.

SPEED

In 1990, the train reached speeds of 320 miles per hour (515 kph).

FEATURES

The TGV is made from aluminium to keep it lightweight.

SIZE

TGV Duplex is 656 feet (200 m) long. It weighs about 380 tons (345 metric tons).

POWER

TGV Duplex runs on electricity. Its eight AC motors can generate about 12,000 horsepower.

TGV Duplex can carry 545 passengers.

TGV Duplex is a double-decker train.

This extreme machine works hard, is very fast, and provides great comfort.

SPEED
6/10

FEATURES
7/10

SIZE
8/10

POWER
6/10

VALUE
9/10

= TOTAL SCORE
36/50

VALUE

The TGV Duplex cost more than $37 million. Its real value is that it lets more passengers travel on a busy route, which could not have handled extra trains.

LOCKHEED SR-71

This military spy plane is the fastest and highest-flying working aircraft ever made. It is known as the **Blackbird** because of its special black paint. The paint soaks up **radar** waves used to find objects in the sky. This plane, therefore, is almost impossible for radar to track.

SPEED

In July 1976, SR-71 set a speed record of 2,193.167 miles per hour (3,529.560 kph). This record is more than three times the speed of sound.

FEATURES

The SR-71 is made of titanium. It has flown to a record height of 16,223 miles (26,108 km). No SR-71 has ever been shot down or hit by enemy fire.

SIZE

This flying giant is 107 feet (33 m) long with a 55-foot (17-m) wingspan. Its loaded weight is 170,000 pounds (77,111 kg).

Lockheed SR-71 is the world's fastest aircraft.

This is the pilot's view inside the cockpit of the SR-71.

POWER

Power is provided by two turbojets that can produce 160,000 horsepower.

VALUE

Each SR-71 costs around $24 million. The U.S. Air Force retired its fleet in 1990 because of high costs. The planes were returned to service briefly in 1997. The last SR-71 flight took place on October 9, 1999.

This incredible flying machine is fast, powerful, and effective. However, in the end, it is just too expensive.

SPEED
9/10

FEATURES
9/10

SIZE
5/10

POWER
8/10

VALUE
6/10

= TOTAL SCORE
37/50

The Antonov An-225 Mriya (a Russian word that means "dream") is the world's largest aircraft. It was built in 1988 to carry the Soviet Union's space shuttle. Only one was ever made. The Soviet space program was **abandoned** after just one flight.

SPEED

The An-225 can fly at a speed of almost 528 miles per hour (850 kph).

FEATURES

The An-225 has six engines. This aircraft was made to carry objects that are too big to fit inside it.

SIZE

The An-225 is 276 feet (84.1 m) long with a 277-foot (84.4-m) wingspan. It weighs 410 tons (372 metric tons) and has a maximum takeoff weight of 661 tons (600 metric tons).

The An-225 carries its cargo in a "piggyback" style.

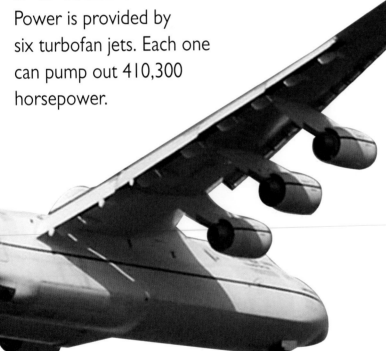

The An-225 has a 32-wheel landing gear.

POWER

Power is provided by six turbofan jets. Each one can pump out 410,300 horsepower.

VALUE

Though it was only used once, this extreme machine cost $30 million.

Only one of these planes has ever been built. There are, however, plans to develop a second.

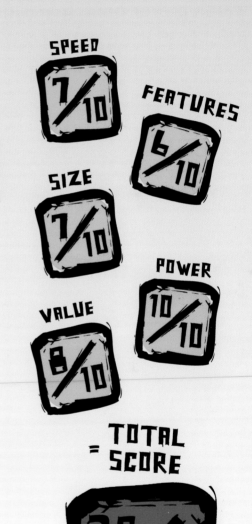

SPEED
7/10

FEATURES
6/10

SIZE
7/10

POWER
10/10

VALUE
8/10

= TOTAL SCORE

38/50

The USS *Ronald Reagan* aircraft carrier is the largest warship ever built. It was named after the 40th U.S. president. It carries a crew of more than 6,000 as well as more than 80 aircraft.

SPEED
The USS *Ronald Reagan* has a top speed of more than 30 knots.

FEATURES
More than a billion parts were used to build the USS *Ronald Reagan*. The warship can sail for more than 20 years before it needs more fuel.

SIZE
This massive vessel is 1,092 feet (333 m) long. It weighs about 100,000 tons (90,718 metric tons). Its flight deck covers more than 4.5 acres (18,211 square meters).

The USS *Ronald Reagan* is almost as long as the Empire State Building is high.

This massive warship weighs more than all the other machines on our list put together. It is the ultimate extreme machine.

SPEED
3/10

FEATURES
10/10

SIZE
10/10

POWER
9/10

VALUE
10/10

= TOTAL SCORE

42/50

This ship is sent all over the world during war and peacetime.

POWER

This huge ship is powered by two nuclear reactors and four steam engines. It produces 260,000 horsepower.

VALUE

The USS *Ronald Reagan* cost $4.5 billion to develop. It is expected to be in service for 50 years. It could prove to be a worthwhile **investment**.

CLOSE
BUT NOT CLOSE ENOUGH

Choosing ten extreme machines for this book was very difficult. Here are five amazing machines that almost made the final list.

SPIRIT OF AUSTRALIA

This powerboat's world record has never been beaten. The *Spirit of Australia* was built by Ken Warby for less than $10,000. On October 8, 1978, Ken and his boat reached a top speed of 317.60 miles per hour (511.11 kph).

THE FA22 RAPTOR

This jet was built to be the world's top fighter plane. It can launch missiles in less than a second. Built for the U.S. Air Force, it cost $258 million. It has a top speed of 1,203 miles per hour (1,936 kph).

THE VOLVO EXTREME GRAVITY CAR

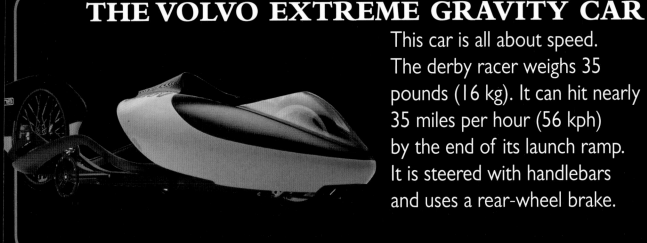

This car is all about speed. The derby racer weighs 35 pounds (16 kg). It can hit nearly 35 miles per hour (56 kph) by the end of its launch ramp. It is steered with handlebars and uses a rear-wheel brake.

NUNA II

This is no UFO. It's the world's fastest **solar**-powered vehicle. Solar cells cover its plastic shell. Nuna II can hit a top speed of 106 miles per hour (171 kph). In October 2003, Nuna II won the World Solar Challenge. It traveled 1,870 miles (3,010 km) in 31 hours and 5 minutes.

BIGFOOT

This is the biggest truck ever built. It is more than 12 feet (3.7 m) tall with tires that weigh 880 pounds (399 kg). Its 1,500 horsepower engine produces a top speed of more than 80 miles per hour (129 kph). A Bigfoot truck can cost between $150,000 and $250,000.

STATS

NO. 10 SHINKAI 6500

Extreme Scores

Speed	2
Features	3
Size	4
Power	3
Value	7

TOTAL SCORE

19 / 50

NO. 9 V-22 OSPREY TILTROTOR

Extreme Scores

Speed	6
Features	4
Size	3
Power	5
Value	7

TOTAL SCORE

25 / 50

NO. 8 LCAC HOVERCRAFT

Extreme Scores

Speed	4
Features	4
Size	6
Power	6
Value	6

TOTAL SCORE

26 / 50

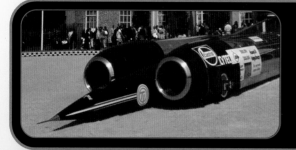

NO. 7 THRUST SSC

Extreme Scores

Speed	8
Features	6
Size	2
Power	8
Value	3

TOTAL SCORE

27 / 50

NO. 6 USS LOUISIANA

Extreme Scores

Speed	3
Features	6
Size	9
Power	7
Value	4

TOTAL SCORE

29 / 50

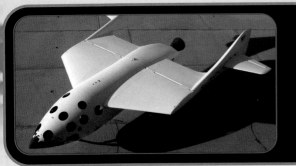

NO. 5 SPACESHIPONE

Extreme Scores

Speed	10
Features	6
Size	2
Power	7
Value	5

TOTAL SCORE

30 / 50

NO. 4 TGV DUPLEX

Extreme Scores

Speed	6
Features	7
Size	8
Power	6
Value	9

TOTAL SCORE

36 / 50

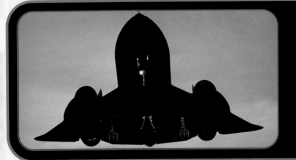

NO. 3 LOCKHEED SR-71

Extreme Scores

Speed	9
Features	9
Size	5
Power	8
Value	6

TOTAL SCORE

37 / 50

NO. 2 ANTONOV AN-225 MRIYA

Extreme Scores

Speed	7
Features	6
Size	7
Power	10
Value	8

TOTAL SCORE

38 / 50

NO. 1 USS RONALD REAGAN

Extreme Scores

Speed	3
Features	10
Size	10
Power	9
Value	10

TOTAL SCORE

42 / 50

GLOSSARY

abandoned (uh-BAN-duhned) no longer used

aircraft (AIR-craft) a vehicle that can fly

amphibious (am-FIB-ee-uhs) able to be used on land and in the water

ballistic (buh-LISS-tik) having to do with weapons that can be fired

critical (KRIT-uh-kuhl) something very serious or dangerous

horsepower (HORSS-pou-ur) the amount of power that a horse can exert; a measurement often used to describe engine power

hovercraft (HUHV-ur-*kraft*) a vehicle that can travel on land and in the water

investment (in-VEST-ment) giving money to something in the belief that you will get more back than what you gave

knots (NOTS) a measurement of speed used for boats and aircraft

manned (MANNED) to have people, usually the crew, on a ship

maximum (MAKS-uh-muhm) the greatest amount possible

nuclear missles (NOO-klee-ur MISS-uhls) very dangerous weapons that are fired and get their destructive energy by splitting atoms

nuclear reactor (NOO-klee-ur ree-AK-tur) a machine that produces energy made by splitting atoms

propeller (pruh-PEL-ur) a spinning blade that is used to help move an aircraft or ship

radar (RAY-dar) a tool used for detecting and finding faraway objects such as aircraft

solar (SOH-lur) having to do with the sun

submarine (SUHB-muh-reen) a ship that can travel under the water as well as on the water's surface

submersible (suhb-MUR-suh-bul) special vehicle designed for deep-sea exploration

supersonic (SOO-pur-SON-ik) traveling faster than the speed of sound

INDEX

A

aircraft 9, 20, 22, 24
aluminium 10, 18
amphibious 10
Antonov An-225 Mriya 22–23, 29

B

Bigfoot 27
Blackbird 20

C

cars 4, 12–13, 27

E

earthquake prediction 7

F

FA22 Raptor 26

H

helicopter 8–9
horsepower 5, 9, 11, 12, 15, 17, 18, 21, 23, 25, 27

J

jet engines 12

K

knots 6, 14, 24

L

landing gear 23
LCAC Hovercraft 10–11, 28
Lockheed SR-71 20–21, 29

M

missiles 14, 26

N

nuclear reactors 14–15, 25
Nuna II 27

P

propeller 9, 14

R

radar waves 20
rocket engine 16–17

S

Shinkai 6500 6–7, 28
solar-powered vehicle 27
sound barrier 12
Soviet Union 22
SpaceShipOne 16–17, 29
Spirit of Australia 26
submarines 14–15
submersible 6–7

T

TGV Duplex 18–19, 29
Thrust SSC 12–13, 28
titanium 7, 20
train 4, 18–19
truck 27

U

U.S. Air Force 8, 21, 26
U.S. Marine Corps 8
U.S. Navy 8, 10, 14
USS Louisiana 14–15, 28
USS Ronald Reagan 24–25, 29

V

Volvo Extreme Gravity Car, The 27
V-22 Osprey Tiltrotor 8–9, 28

W

warship 24
White Knight jet 16–17